PROMISES
for Growing Christians

James Ryan

BROADMAN PRESS
Nashville, Tennessee

© Copyright 1985 • Broadman Press
All Rights Reserved
4250-14
ISBN: 0-8054-5014-9

Dewey Decimal Classification: 248
Subject Heading: SPIRITUAL LIFE
Library of Congress Catalog Number:
84-22953
Printed in the United States of America

Library of Congress Cataloging in Publication Data

Ryan, James, 1940-
  Bible promises for growing Christians

  1. Christian life 2. Christian
life—Bilical teaching. I. Title.
BV4501.2.R87 1985   242'.5   84-22953
ISBN 0-8054-5014-9 (pak.)

Contents

Introduction
  I. **God's Promises and Your Salvation in Christ. . . 7**
  II. **God's Promises and Your Daily Walk with Christ. . . 11**

        Anger. . . 11
        Assurance. . . 12
        Bible Study. . . 12
        Character. . . 13
        Cheerfulness. . . 14
        Christ. . . 15
        Church Attendance. . . 16
        Consecration. . . 18
        Courage. . . 18
        Death. . . 20
        Discouragement. . . 21
        Doubts. . . 22
        Duty. . . 23
        Faith. . . 24
        Forgiveness. . . 25
        Friendship. . . 26
        Giving. . . 27
        Gratitude. . . 28
        Growth. . . 29
        Happiness. . . 30
        Happy Home. . . 31
        Health. . . 32
        Heaven. . . 33
        Hell. . . 34
        Holy Spirit. . . 36
        Hope. . . 37
        Humility. . . 38
        Joy. . . 38

Judgment... 39
Love... 40
Obeying God... 42
Patience... 43
Peace... 44
Prayer... 45
Reward... 46
Service... 48
Sin... 49
Soul-winning... 50
Speech... 51
Strength... 52
Success... 54
Suffering... 55
Temptation... 56
Time... 57
Truthfulness... 58
Worship... 59

III. **God's Promises Through Spiritual Exercises... 64**
How to Have a Quiet Time with God... 64
How to Pray... 65
How to Find God's Will in Your Life... 67
How to Lead a Person to Christ... 68
How to Memorize Scriptures... 70
Scripture Memory... 72
How to Get Along with Others... 76
How to Live Through Difficult Times... 77
How to Get the Most out of Life... 79

Introduction

This promise book draws together great promises from throughout the Bible—promises that help you understand God's loving plan for your life.

Each section gives Scriptures from throughout the Bible to suggest that God's promises have been constant throughout the ages. Whatever the particular needs of persons have been, God has always been there to help in time of need. God's love flows from generation to generation.

God is love. (1 John 4:8) Jesus said, "Greater love hath no man than this, that a man lay down his life for his friends" (John 15:13). God loves you. God's greatest demonstration of love and greatest promise to you is fulfilled in Christ's death on the cross.

God so loves us that He gave His only begotten Son, that when anyone believes on Him that person shall not perish but have everlasting life (John 3:16).

When you allowed Christ in your life, you became a inheritor of God's richest promises. You are God's child. Everlasting life is yours. The abundant life is yours. All the promises you need to make your daily walk a heavenly journey can now be fulfilled. Claim the ones you need today.

There are thousands of distinct promises in the Word of God. This believers' promise book lists more than 400 of the richest.

I
God's Promises and Your Salvation in Christ

Chapter one of this promise book is designed to help you think through your own personal salvation experience. Everyone has needs—physical, mental, social, and spiritual. This is a book to help you meet your spiritual needs.

Much is said in the New Testament about the necessity and technique of spiritual growth. This suggests that persons have a basic spiritual need —salvation—and that the Christian life is a walk toward maturity in our salvation. Our need is salvation. Our goal is maturity in *Christ*. Follow the three basic steps toward assurance of eternal life through Christ.

I. Repentance involves a turning from sin toward God.
1. Let the wicked forsake his way, and the unrighteous man his thoughts: and let him return unto the Lord, and he will have mercy on him; and to our God, for he will abundantly pardon (Isa. 55:7).
2. They shall come with weeping, and with supplications will I lead them. (Jer. 31:9).
3. But if the wicked will turn from all his sins that he hath committed, . . . he shall surely live, he shall not die (Ezek. 18:21).
4. Turn ye unto me, saith the Lord of hosts, and I will turn unto you, saith the Lord of hosts (Zech. 1:3).
5. Blessed are they that mourn: for they shall be comforted. (Matt. 5:4).
6. Repent ye therefore, and be converted, that your sins may be blotted out, when the times of refreshing shall come from the

presence of the Lord (Acts 3:19).
7. The Lord is nigh unto them that are of a broken heart; and saveth such as be of a contrite spirit (Ps. 34:18).
8. For godly sorrow worketh repentance to salvation (2 Cor. 7:10).
9. Repent, and be baptized every one of you in the name of Jesus Christ for the remisson of sins, and ye shall receive the gift of the Holy Ghost (Acts 2:38).

Write your definition of repentance.
What did you do when you repented?
How did you feel when you repented?
Write God's promise you want to memorize.

If you have not repented of your sins and would like to do so, bow your head and claim these promises right now. As a person repents and decides to accept the Lordship of Christ in his life, he receives everlasting forgiveness for his sins.

As a Christian grows she soon realizes a continuing need for repentance. Each day a Christian must repent, ask God's forgiveness for daily transgressions and review her committment to God. This is an ongoing process.

On a separate sheet of paper, write the sins which burden you today. Let God carry the load.

II. Belief involves placing your trust in one who is thought to be trustworthy.
1. And they said, *Believe* on the Lord Jesus Christ and thou shalt be saved (Acts 16:31).
2. Therefore I say unto you, what things soever ye desire, when ye pray, *believe* that ye receive them, and ye shall have them (Mark 11:24).

Your Salvation in Christ

3. He that *believeth* and is baptized shall be saved; but he that believeth not shall be damned. (Mark 16:16).
4. But as many as received him, to them gave he power to become the sons of God, even to them that *believe* on his name (John 1:12).
5. For God so loved the world, that he gave his only begotten Son, that whoever *believeth* in him should not perish, but have everlasting life (John 3:16).
6. He that believeth on him is not condemned: but he that *believeth* not is condemned already, because he hath not believed in the name of the only begotten Son of God (John 3:18).
7. He that believeth on the Son hath everlasting life: and he that *believeth* not the Son shall not see life; but the wrath of God abideth on him (John 6:47).
8. He that heareth my word, and *believeth* on him that sent me, hast everlasting life, and shall not come into condemnation; but is passed from death unto life (John 5:24).

Write your definition of belief.

What did you believe when you believed?

Write God's promise that you would like to memorize.

Belief involves action. It means trust and commitment. God invites you to place your trust in Him—in His ability to forgive you of your sin and give you everlasting life. God never fails. Repentance and belief are twin words for the Christian. Repentance without belief in God's promises of forgiveness and eternal life would be meaningless. Belief without sincere repentance for sins against God implies unwillingness to relate to a sinless God. The whole purpose of forgiveness is to enjoy God's friendship.

III. Confession involves public acknowledgment

of Christ.
1. ... I will *confess* my transgressions unto the Lord: and thou forgavest the iniquity of my sin (Ps. 32:5).
2. He that covereth his sins shall not prosper: but whoso *confesseth* and forsaketh them shall have mercy (Prov. 28:13).
3. Whosoever therefore shall *confess* me before men, him will I confess also before my Father which is in heaven (Matt. 10:32).
4. Whosoever shall confess me before men, him shall the Son of man also *confess* before the angels of God (Luke 12:8).
5. ... he that *acknowledgeth* the Son hath the Father also (1 John 2:23).
6. That if thou shalt *confess* with thy mouth the Lord Jesus, and shalt believe in thine heart that God hath raised him from the dead, thou shalt be saved (Rom. 10:9).
7. If we *confess* our sins, he is faithful and just to forgive us our sins, and to cleanse us from all unrighteousness (1 John 1:9).
8. Whosoever shall *confess* that Jesus is the Son of God, God dwelleth in him, and he in God. 1 John 4:15
9. And Simon Peter (confessed) answered and said, Thou art the Christ, the Son of the living God . . . (Jesus said) and I will give unto thee the keys of the kingdom of heaven (Matt. 16:16,19*a*).

Write your definition of confession

What is the purpose of confession?

Write Romans 10:9 and memorize this promise. Do you see the connection between "belief" and "confession"?

Confession implies public acknowledgement. Jesus requires all His followers to publicly state their belief in Him as the Savior from their sins and Lord of their lives.

II
God's Promises and Your Daily Walk with Christ

Anger

I find it difficult to control my temper. What does God say?

Cease from *anger,* and forsake wrath: . . . those that wait upon the Lord, they shall inherit the earth (Ps. 37: 8-9).

A soft answer turneth away wrath: but grievious words stir up anger (Prov. 15:1).

He that is slow to anger is better than the mighty; and he that ruleth his spirit than he that taketh a city (Prov. 16:32).

The discretion (good sense) of a man deferreth his anger; and it is his glory to pass over a trangression (Prov. 19:11).

He that hath no rule over his own spirit is like a city that is broken down, and without walls (Prov. 25:28).

Be not hasty in thy spirit to be angry: for anger resteth in the bosom of fools (Eccl. 7:9).

Whosoever is angry with his brother without a cause shall be in danger of the judgment (Matt. 5:22 *a*).

Be ye angry, and sin not: let not the sun go down upon your wrath . . . Let all . . . anger . . . be put away from you, . . . forgiving one another, even as God for Christ's sake hath forgiven you (Eph. 4:26,31 *a,*32 *b*).

Assurance

How can I be assured of my salvation even when I backslide?

For our gospel came not unto you in word only, but also in power, and in the Holy Ghost, and in much assurance (1 Thess. 1:5).
. . . I know whom I have believed, and am persuaded that he is able to keep that which I have committed unto him against that day (2 Tim. 1:12).
Let us draw near with a true heart in full assurance of faith . . . (Heb. 10:22).
And hereby we do know that we know him, if we keep his commandments (1 John 2:3).
Hereby know we that we dwell in him, and he in us, because he hath given us of his Spirit (1 John 4:13).
And will be a Father unto you, and ye shall be my sons and daughters, saith the Lord almighty (2 Cor. 6:18).
But know that the Lord hath set apart him that is godly for himself: the Lord will hear when I call unto him (Ps. 4:3).
According as he hath chosen us in him before the foundation of the world, that one should be holy and without blame before him in love (Eph. 1:4).
If God be for us, who can be against us? (Rom. 8:31).

Bible Study

Is daily Bible study necessary?

The grass withereth, the flower fadeth; but the word of our God shall stand for ever (Isa. 40:8).
For verily I say unto you, Till heaven and earth

Your Daily Walk with Christ

pass, one jot or one tittle shall in no wise pass from the law, till all be fulfilled (Matt. 5:18).

... man doth not live by bread only, but by every word that proceedeth out of the mouth of the Lord doth man live (Deut. 8:3).

Thy words were found, and I did eat them; and thy word was unto me the joy and rejoicing of mine heart; . . . (Jer. 15:16).

As newborn babes, desire the sincere milk of the word, that ye may grow thereby (1 Pet. 2:2).

All Scripture is given by inspiration of God, and is profitable for doctrine, for reproof, for correction, for instruction in righteousness (2 Tim. 3:16).

And these words, which I command thee this day, shall be in thine heart (Deut. 6:6).

Thy word have I hid in mine heart, that I might not sin against thee (Ps. 119:11).

The statutes of the Lord are right, rejoicing the heart: the commandment of the Lord is pure, enlightening the eyes (Ps. 19:8).

For whatsoever things were written aforetime were written for our learning, that we through patience and comfort of the scriptures might have hope (Rom. 15:4).

Search the scriptures, for in them ye think we have eternal life: and they are they which testify of me (John 5:39).

Character

Do I change when I become a follower of Christ?

And God said, Let us make man in our image, after our likeness . . . so God created man in his own image, . . . and God blessed them, and God said unto them, Be fruitful and multiply, and replenish the earth and subdue it: and have dominion over the fish of the sea, and over the fowl of the air, and over every living thing that moveth upon the earth (Gen. 1:26-28).

What is man, that thou art mindful of him? . . . For thou hast made him a little lower than the angels, and hast crowned him with glory and honor. Thou madest him to have dominion over the works of thy hands (Ps. 8:4-6).

. . . whatsoever things are true, whatsoever things are honest, whatsoever things are just, whatsoever things are pure, whatsoever things are lovely, whatsoever things are of good report; if there be any virture, and if there be any praise, think on these things . . . Those things, . . . do: and the God of peace shall be with you (Phil. 4:8-9).

For the grace of God that bringeth salvation hath appeared to all men. Teaching us that, denying ungodliness and worldly lusts, we should live soberly, righteously, and godly in this present world; . . . that he might redeem us from all integrity, and purify unto himself a peculiar people, zealous of good works (Titus 2:11-14).

For we are his workmanship, created in Christ Jesus unto good works, which God hath before ordained that we should walk in them (Eph. 2:10).

Cheerfulness

Sometimes I'm cheerful, sometimes not. What does God say?

. . . let thy heart cheer thee in the days of thy youth, and walk in the ways of thine heart, and in the sight of thine eyes: but know thou, that for all these things God will bring thee into judgment (Eccl. 11:9).

. . . In the world ye shall have tribulation: but be of good cheer; I have overcome the world (John 16:33).

Your Daily Walk with Christ

Wherefore, sirs, be of good cheer: For I believe God (Acts 27:25).

. . . God loveth a cheerful giver (2 Cor. 9:7).

. . . He that giveth, let him do it with simplicity; he that ruleth, with diligence; he that showeth mercy, with cheerfulness (Rom. 12:8).

A merry heart maketh a cheerful countenance (Prov. 15:13).

. . . he that is of a merry heart hath a continual feast. (Prov. 15:15).

A merry heart doeth good like a medicine (Prov. 17:22).

. . . whoso trusteth in the Lord, happy is he (Prov. 16:20).

Where there is no vision, the people perish: but he that keepeth the law, happy is he (Prov. 29:-18).

But and if ye suffer for righteousness sake, happy are ye (1 Pet. 3:14).

Christ

Is Christ really the Son of God. What does this mean to me?

. . . know assuredly, that God hath made Jesus, . . . both Lord and Christ (Acts 2:36).

. . . We also joy in God through our Lord Jesus Christ by whom we have received the atonement (Rom. 5:11).

And if Christ be in you, the body is dead because of sin, but the Spirit is life because of righteousness (Rom. 8:10).

For Christ is the end of the law for righteousness to every one that believeth (Rom. 10:4).

For to this end Christ both died, and rose, and revived, that he might be Lord both of the dead and living (Rom. 14:9).

And ye are Christ's; and Christ is God's (1 Cor. 3:23).

For since by man came death, by man came also the reserrection of the dead. For as in Adam all die, even so in Christ shall all be made alive (1 Cor. 15:21-22).

And because ye are sons, God hath sent forth the Spirit of his Son into your hearts, crying, Abba, Father. Wherefore thou art no more a servant but a son and if a son, then an heir of God through Christ (Gal. 4:6-7).

When Christ, who is our life, shall appear, then shall ye also appear with him in glory (Col. 3:4).

And this is the promise that he hath promised us, even eternal life (1 John 2:25).

Whosoever believeth that Jesus is the Christ is born of God: (1 John 5:1).

To him give all the prophets witness, that through his name whosoever believeth in him shall receive remission of sins (Acts 10:43).

Unto the Son he saith, Thy throne, O God, is for ever and ever (Heb. 1:8).

He is able also to save them to the uttermost that come unto God by him, seeing he ever liveth to make intercession for them (Heb. 7:25).

For there is one God, and one mediator between God and men, the man Christ Jesus (1 Tim. 2:5).

Church Attendance

Why should I attend Church regularly?

Let us hold fast the profession of our faith without wavering; (for he is faithful that promised;) . . . Not forsaking the assembling of ourselves together, as the manner of some is; but exhorting one another: and so much the more, as ye see the day approaching (Heb. 10:23,25).

Those that be planted in the house of the Lord shall flourish in the courts of our God (Ps. 92:13).

Blessed be he that cometh in the name of the

Your Daily Walk with Christ

Lord: We have blessed you out of the house of the Lord (Ps. 118:26).

I was glad when they said unto me, let us go into the house of the Lord . . . because of the house of the Lord our God I will seek thy good (Ps. 122:1,9).

. . . the church of the living God, the pillar and ground of the truth (1 Tim 3:15).

And he (Jesus) came to Nazareth, where he had been brought up: and, as his custom was, he went into the synagogue on the sabbath day, and stood up for to read.

> The Spirit of the Lord is upon me, because he hath anointed me to preach the gospel to the poor; he hath sent one to heal the brokenhearted, to preach deliverance to the captives, and recovering of sight to the blind, to set at liberty them that are bruised, To preach the acceptable year of the Lord. . . .

and he began to say unto them, this day is this scripture fulfilled in your ears (Luke 4: 16,18-19,21).

Blessed are they that dwell in thy house: they will still be praising thee (Ps. 84:4).

One thing have I desired of the Lord, that will I seek after; that I may dwell in the house of the Lord all the days of my life, to behold the beauty of the Lord, and to enquire in his temple. For in the time of trouble he shall hide me in his pavilion: in the secret of his tabernacle shall he hide me; he shall set me up upon a rock. And now shall mine head be lifted up above mine enemies round about me: therefore will I offer in his tabernacle sacrifices of joy; I will sing, yea, I will sing praises unto the Lord (Ps. 27:4-6).

Consecration

What does consecration involve? What does God require of me?

I beseech you therefore, brethren, by the mercies of God, that ye present your bodies a living sacrifice, holy, acceptable unto God, which is your reasonable service. And be not conformed to this world: But be ye transformed by the renewing of your mind, that ye may prove what is that good, and acceptable, and perfect will of God (Rom. 12:1-2).

. . . ye are the temple of the living God; as God hath said, I will dwell in them, and walk in them; and I will be their God, and they shall be my people (2 Cor. 6:16*b*).

But ye are a chosen generation, a royal priesthood, an holy nation, a peculiar people; that ye should show forth the praises of him who hath called you out of darkness into his marvelous light: (1 Peter 2:9).

But the anointing which ye have received of him abideth in you, and ye need not that any man teach you: But as the same anointing teacheth you of all things, and is truth, and is no lie, and even as it hath taught you, ye shall abide in him (1 John 2:27).

He that overcometh shall inherit all things; and I will be his God, and he shall be my son (Rev. 21:7).

As ye have therefore received Christ Jesus the Lord, so walk ye in him: Rooted and built up in him (Col. 2:6-7).

Courage

Can God take away my fears in this uncertain world?

Your Daily Walk with Christ

Wait on the Lord: Be of good courage, and he shall strengthen thine heart: wait, I say, on the Lord (Ps. 27:14).

Be strong and of a good courage, fear not, nor be afraid of them: For the Lord thy God, he it is that doth go with thee; he will not fail thee, nor forsake thee (Deut. 31:6).

. . . Deal courageously, and the Lord shall be with the good (2 Chron. 19:11).

And in nothing terrified by your adversaries which is to them an evident token of perdition, but you of salvation, and that of God (Phil. 1:28).

Finally my brethren, be strong in the Lord, and in the power of his might. Put on the whole armor of God, that ye may be able to stand against the wiles of the devil. For we wrestle not against flesh and blood, but against principalities, against powers, against the rulers of the darkness of this world, against spiritual wickedness in high places. Wherefore take unto you the whole armor of God, that ye may be able to withstand in the evil day . . . (Eph. 6:10-13).

Thou therefore, my son, be strong in the grace that is in Christ Jesus . . . If we suffer, we shall also reign with him; if we deny him, he also will deny us: (2 Tim. 2:1,12).

The Lord is my light and my salvation; whom shall I fear? The Lord is the strength of my life; of whom shall I be afraid? (Ps. 27:1).

The Lord is on my side; I will not fear: What can man do unto me? (Ps. 118:6).

Behold, God is my salvation; I will trust, and not be afraid: for the Lord Jehovah is my strength and my song; he also is become my salvation. (Isa. 12:2).

. . . If God be for us, who can be against us? He that spared not his own Son, but delivered him up for us all, how shall he not with him also freely give us all things? (Rom. 8:31-32).

Be of good courage, and he shall strengthen your heart, all ye that hope in the Lord (Ps. 31:24).

I sought the Lord, and he heard me, and delivered me from all my fears (Ps. 34:4).

Death

What is the Christian view of death?

And as it is appointed unto men once to die, but after this the judgement: So Christ was once offered to bear the sins of many: And unto them that look for him shall he appear . . . (Heb. 9:27-28).

Wherefore, as by one man sin entered into the world, and death by sin; and so death passed upon all men, for that all have sinned: . . . that as sin hath reigned unto death, even so might grace reign through righteousness unto eternal life by Jesus Christ Our Lord (Rom. 5:12,21).

The sting of death is sin; . . . But thanks be to God, which giveth us the victory through our Lord Jesus Christ (1 Cor. 15:56,57).

. . . Blessed are the dead which die in the Lord from henceforth: yea, saith the Spirit, that they may rest from their labors; and their works do follow them (Rev. 14:13).

For to me to live is Christ, and to die is gain (Phil. 1:21).

For I am now ready to be offered, and the time of my departure is at hand. I have fought a good fight, I have finished my course, I have kept the faith: Henceforth there is laid up for me a crown of righteousness, which the Lord, the righteous judge shall give me at that day: and not to me only, but unto all them also that love his appearing (2 Tim. 4:6-8).

For that which befalleth the sons of men be-

falleth beasts; even one thing befalleth them: as the one dieth, so dieth the other; . . . all are of the dust, and all turn to dust again. Who knoweth the spirit of man that goeth upward and the spirit of the beast that goeth downward to earth? (Eccl. 3:19-21).
But I would not have you to be ignorant, brethren, concerning them which are asleep, that ye sorrow not, even as others which have no hope. For if we believe that Jesus died and rose again, even so them also which sleep in Jesus will God bring with him (1 Thess. 4:13-14).
For we know that if our earthly house of this tabernacle were dissolved, we have a building of God, an house not made with hands, eternal in the heavens (2 Cor. 5:1).

Discouragement

I get bogged down with daily discouragements. Can reading the Bible help?

Why art thou cast down, O my soul? and why art thou disquieted within me? hope in God: for I shall yet praise him, who is the health of my countenance, and my God (Ps. 43:5).
Woe is me! . . . The good man is perished out of the earth: and there is none upright among men: they all lie in wont for blood; they hunt every man his brother with a net. That they may do evil with both hands earnestly, . . . Therefore I will look unto the Lord: I will wait for the God of my salvation: my God will hear me (Mic. 7:1,2-3,7).
Hope deferred maketh the heart sick: but when the desire cometh, it is a tree of life (Prov. 13:12).
But as for me, my feet were almost gone; my steps had well nigh slipped. For I was envious at the foolish, when I saw the prosperity of the wicked . . . My flesh and my heart faileth: But

God is the strength of my heart, and my portion for ever (Ps. 73:2-3,26).

... The Lord hath forsaken me, and my Lord hath forgotten me. Can a woman forget her sucking child, that she should not have compassion on the son of her womb? Yea, they may forget, yet will I (The Lord) not forget thee (Isa. 49:14-15).

Behold, the Lord God will help me; who is he that shall condemn me? (Isa. 50:9).

Strangers are risen up against me, and oppressors seek after my soul ... Behold, God is mine helper (Ps. 54:3-4).

... My strength and my hope is perished from the Lord: Remembering mine affliction and my misery, ... It is of the Lord's mercies that we are not consumed, because his compassions fail not. They are new every morning: great is thy faithfulness (Lam. 3:18-19,22-23).

And the Lord, he it is that doth go before thee; he will be with thee, he will not fail thee, nor forsake thee: Fear not, neither be dismayed (Deut. 31:8).

Doubts

Even though I believe in a God who is personal and powerful, sometimes doubts creep in. How do I deal with these doubts?

If ye have faith and doubt not, ye shall say unto this mountain, Be thou removed, and be thou cast into the sea; it shall be done. And all things, whatsoever ye shall ask in prayer, believing, ye shall receive (Matt. 21:21-22).

Have faith in God. For verily I say unto you, that whosoever shall say unto this mountain, Be thou removed, and be thou cast into the sea; and shall not doubt in his heart, but shall believe that those things which he saith shall come to pass;

Your Daily Walk with Christ

he shall have whatsoever he saith (Mark 11:22-23).

And seek not ye what ye shall eat, or what ye shall drink, neither be ye of doubtful mind. For all these things do the nations of the world seek after: and your Father knoweth that ye have need of these things. But rather seek ye the kingdom of God; and all these things shall be added unto you (Luke 12:29-31).

Jesus saith unto him, Thomas, because thou hast seen me, thou hast believed: blessed are they that have not seen, and yet have believed (John 20:-29).

Let us hold fast the profession of our faith without wavering; for he is faithful that promised (Heb. 10:23).

For I know that my redeemer liveth, and that he shall stand at the latter day upon the earth (Job 19:25).

. . . for I know whom I have believed, and am persuaded that he is able to keep that which I have committed unto him against that day (2 Tim. 1:12).

Duty

I don't want my Christian service to be only a matter of duty. What does duty really mean?

And he said to them all, If any man will come after me, let him deny himself, and take up his cross daily, and follow me. For whosoever will save his life shall lose it: but whosoever will lose his life for my sake, the same shall save it (Luke 9:23-24).

For I was an hungered, and ye gave me meat; I was thirsty, and ye gave me drink: I was a stranger, and ye took me in: Naked, and ye clothed me: I was sick, and ye visited me: I was in prison, and ye came unto me. Brethren, ye have done it unto me (Matt. 25:35-36,40).

I have showed you all things, how that so laboring ye ought to support the weak, and to remember the words of the Lord Jesus, how he said, It is more blessed to give than to receive (Acts 20:35).

We then that are strong ought to bear the infirmities of the weak, and not to please ourselves . . . that, we through patience and comfort of the Scriptures might have hope (Rom. 15:1,4).

For whosoever will save his life shall lose it: and whosoever will lose his life shall find it (Matt. 16:25).

As every man hath received the gift, even so minister the same one to another, as good stewards of the manifold grace of God. . . . If any man minister, let him do it as of the ability which God giveth: (1 Pet. 4:10-11).

. . . I am made all things to all men, that I might by all means save some (1 Cor. 9:22).

. . . Fear God, and keep his commandments: For this is the whole duty of man. For God shall bring every work into judgements, with every thing, whether it be good, or whether it be evil (Eccl. 12:13-14).

Faith

What is faith? What will it do for me?

Now faith is the substance of things hoped for, the evidence of things not seen . . . Through faith we understand that the worlds were framed by the word of God (Heb. 11:1,3).

But without faith it is impossible to please him: for he that cometh to God must believe that he is, and that he is a rewarder of them that diligently seek him (Heb. 11:6).

And Jesus said unto them, . . . verily I say unto

Your Daily Walk with Christ

you, if ye have faith as a grain of mustard seed, ye shall say unto this mountain, Remove hence to yonder place; and it shall remove: and nothing shall be impossible unto you (Matt. 17:20).

Commit thy way unto the Lord; trust also in him; and he shall bring it to pass (Ps. 37:5).

Many sorrows shall be to the wicked: but he that trusteth in the Lord, mercy shall compass him about (Ps. 32:10).

They that trust in the Lord shall be as mount Zion, which cannot be removed, but abideth for ever (Ps. 125:1).

The fear of man bringeth a snare: but whoso putteth his trust in the Lord shall be safe (Prov. 29:25).

Blessed is the man that trusteth in the Lord, and whose hope the Lord is (Jer. 17:7).

The Lord is good, a strong hold in the day of trouble; and he knoweth them that trust in him (Nah. 1:7).

Thou wilt keep him in perfect peace, whose mind is stayed on thee: because he trusteth in thee (Isa. 26:3).

Trust in the Lord with all thine heart; and lean not unto thine own understanding. In all thy ways acknowledge him, and he shall direct thy paths (Prov. 3:5-6).

Forgiveness

I know God forgives me. I find it difficult to forgive others.

For if ye forgive men their tresspasses, your heavenly Father will also forgive you: (Matt. 6:14).

And be ye kind one to another, tenderhearted, forgiving one another, even as God for Christ's sake hath forgiven you (Eph. 4:32).

Therefore if thine enemy hunger, feed him; if he

thirst, give him drink: for in so doing thou shalt heap coals of fire on his head (Rom. 12:20).

And unto him that smiteth thee on the one cheek offer also the other (Luke 6:29).

But love ye your enemies and do good, and lend, hoping for nothing again; and your reward shall be great, and ye shall be the children of the highest: for he is king unto the unthankful and to the evil (Luke 6:35).

Say not thou, I will recompense evil; but wait on the Lord, and he shall save thee (Prov. 20:22).

Not rendering evil for evil, or railing for railing, but contrariwise blessing: knowing that ye are thereunto called, that ye should inherit a blessing (1 Peter 3:9).

Blessed are the merciful: for they shall obtain mercy (Matt. 5:7).

Therefore thou art inexcusable, O man, whosoever thou art that judgest: for wherein thou judgest another, thou condemnest thyself; . . . (Rom. 2:1).

Judge not, that ye be not judged (Matt. 7:1).

Friendship

I do not feel friendly toward everyone with whom I come in contact. What does God say?

Two are better than one; because they have a good reward for their labor. For if they fall, the one will lift up his fellow: but woe to him that is alone when he falleth; for he hath not another to help him up (Eccl. 4:9-10).

A man that hath friends must show himself friendly: and there is a friend that sticketh closer than a brother (Prov. 18:24).

Greater love hath no man than this, that a man lay down his life for his friends. Ye are my friends, if ye do whatsoever I command you. Henceforth I call you not servants; for the servant knoweth not what his Lord doeth; but I have called you friends; for all things that I have heard of my Father I have made known unto you. These things I command you, that ye love one another (John 15:13-15,17).

He that loveth his brother abideth in the light, and there is none occasion of stumbling in him (1 John 2:10).

We know that we have passed from death unto life, because we love the brethren (1 John 3:14).

Owe no man anything, but to love another: for he that loveth another hath fulfilled the law (Rom. 13:8).

Giving (Stewardship)

It is difficult for me to give to God and others. What does God require?

Will a man rob God? Yet ye have robbed me. But ye say, wherin have we robbed thee? In tithes and offerings (Mal. 3:8).

Bring ye all the tithes into the storehouse, that there may be meat in mine house, and prove me now herewith, saith the Lord of hosts, if I will not open you the windows of heaven, and pour you out a blessing, that there shall not be room enough to receive it (Mal. 3:10).

Woe unto you, scribes and pharisies, hypocrites! for ye pay tithe of mint and anise and cummin, and have omitted the weightier matters of the law, judgment, mercy, and faith: these ought ye to have done, and not to leave the others undone ... Thou blind pharisee, cleanse first that which is within the cup and platter, that the outside of them may be clean also (Matt. 23:23,26).

He that giveth unto the poor shall not lack: but he that hideth his eyes shall have many a curse (Prov. 28:27).

Everyman according as he purposeth in his

heart, so let him give; not grudgingly, or of necessity: for God loveth a cheerful giver. (2 Cor. 9:7).

Every man shall give as he is able, according to the blessing of the Lord thy God which he hath given thee (Deut. 16:17).

Honor the Lord with thy substance, and with the firstfruits of all thine increase: So shall thy barns be filled with plenty, and thy presses shall burst out with new wine (Prov. 3:9-10).

And Jesus sat over against the treasury, and beheld how the people cast money into the treasury: and many that were rich cast in much. And there came a certain poor widow, and she threw in two mites, which make a farthing. And he called unto him his disciples, and saith unto them, Verily I say unto you, that this poor widow hath cast more in than all they which have cast into the treasury: For all they did cast in of their abundance; but she of her want did cast in all that she had, even all her living (Mark 12:41-44).

Upon the first day of the week let every one of you lay by him in store, as God hath prospered him, that there be no gatherings when I come (1 Cor. 16:2).

Gratitude

Why should I be thankful to God? Life is pretty tough.

In every thing give thanks: for this is the will of God in Christ Jesus concerning you (1 Thess. 5:18).

Serve the Lord with gladness: come before his presence with singing. Enter into his gates with thanksgiving, and into his courts with praise: be thankful unto him, and bless his name. For the

Your Daily Walk with Christ

Lord is good; his mercy is everlasting; and his truth endureth to all generations (Ps. 100:2,4-5). Bless the Lord, O my soul, and forget not all his benefits: who forgiveth all thine iniquities; who healeth all thy diseases (Ps. 103:2-3).

But thanks be to God, which giveth us the victory through our Lord Jesus Christ (1 Cor. 15:57).

... Blessed be the name of God for ever and ever: for wisdom and might are his; and he changeth the tunes and the seasons: he removeth kings and setteth up kings: he giveth wisdom unto the wise, and knowledge to them that know understanding: he revealeth the deep and secret things: he knoweth what is in the darkness, and the light dwelleth with him (Dan. 2:20-22).

The Lord preserveth all them that love him: ... my mouth shall speak the praise of the Lord: and let all flesh bless his holy name for ever and ever (Ps. 145:20-21).

Oh that men would praise the Lord for his goodness, and for his wonderful works to the children of men (Ps. 107:8).

But I will sacrifice unto thee with the voice of thanksgiving; I will pay that that I have vowed. Salvation is of the Lord (Jonah 2:9).

Growth

I want to grow as a Christian. Show me how.

Every branch in me that beareth not fruit he taketh away: and every branch that beareth fruit, he purgeth it, that it may bring forth more fruit ... abide in me, and I in you. As the branch cannot bear fruit of itself, except it abide in the vine; no more can ye, except ye abide in me. I am the vine, ye are the branches: He that abideth in me, and I in him, the same bringeth forth much fruit (John 15:2,4-5).

As newborn babes, desire the sincere milk of the

word, that ye may grow thereby: . . . ye also, as lively stones are built up a spiritual house, a holy priesthood, to offer up spiritual sacrifices, acceptable to God by Jesus Christ (1 Pet. 2:2,5). And beside this, giving all diligence, add to your faith virtue, and to virtue knowledge; and to knowledge temperance; and to temperance patience; and to patience godliness; and to godliness brotherly kindness; and to brotherly kindness charity. For if these things be in you, and abound, they make you that ye shall neither be barren nor unfruitful in the knowledge of our Lord Jesus Christ (2 Pet. 1:5-8).

. . . he which hath begun a good work in you will perform it until the day of Jesus Christ: (Phil. 1:6).

That we henceforth be no more children, tossed to and fro, and carried about with every wind of doctrine, by the sleight of men, and cunning craftiness, whereby they lie in wait to deceive; But speaking the truth in love, may grow up into him in all things, which is the head, even Christ: From whom the whole body fitly joined together and compacted by that which every joint supplieth, according to the effectual working in the measure of every part, maketh increase of the body unto the edifying of itself in love (Eph. 4:14-16).

Happiness

I want to be happy. Is there a way in this world to be really happy?

Blessed are the poor in spirit: for theirs is the kingdom of heaven. Blessed are they that mourn: for they shall be comforted. Blessed are the meek: for they shall inherit the earth. Blessed are they which do hunger and thirst after righteousness: for they shall be filled. Blessed are the merciful: for they shall obtain mercy. Blessed are the pure in heart: for they shall see God. Blessed are the peacemakers: for they shall be called the children of God. Blessed are they which are persecuted for righteousness' sake: for theirs is the kingdom of heaven. Blessed are ye, when men shall revile you, and persecute you, and shall say all manner of evil against you falsely, for my sake. Rejoice, and be exceeding glad: for great is your reward in heaven (Matt. 5:3-12).

Happy Home

Happiness in the home is God's plan and everyone's desire. What does the Bible say?

But if any provide not for his own, and especially for those of his own house, he hath denied the faith, and is worse than an infidel (1 Tim. 5:8).
. . . the good works of some are manifest before hand; and they that are otherwise cannot be hid (1 Tim. 5:25).
Train up a child in the way he should go: and when he is old, he will not depart from it (Prov. 22:6).
For he . . . appointed a law . . . which he commanded our fathers, that they should make known to their children: That they might set their hope in God, and not forget the works of God, but keep his commandments: (Ps. 78:5,7).
For I have told him that I will judge his house for ever for the iniquity he knoweth; because his sons made themselves vile, and he restrained them not (1 Sam. 3:13).
The father of the righteous shall greatly rejoice: and he that begetteth a wise child shall have joy of him (Prov. 23:24).
Correct thy son, and he shall give thee rest; yet, he shall give delight unto thy soul (Prov. 29:17).

Except the Lord build the house, they labour in vain that build it: . . . (Ps. 127:1).

Lo, children are an heritage of the Lord: and the fruit of the womb is his reward. As arrow are in the hand of a mighty man; so are children of the youth. Happy is the man that hath his quiver full of them (Ps. 127:3-5).

Honor thy father and mother which is the first commandment with promise; that it may be well with thee, and thou mayest live long on the earth (Eph. 6:2-3).

Children, obey your parents in all things: for this is well pleasing unto the Lord (Col. 3:20).

Whoso findeth a wife findeth a good thing, and obtaineth favour of the Lord (Prov. 18:22).

Marriage is honorable in all, and the bed undefiled: but whoremongers and adulterers God will judge (Heb. 13:4).

A foolish son is a grief to his father, and bitterness to her that bare him (Prov. 17:25).

Health

Is it important for me to take care of my body?

Know ye not that ye are the temple of God, and that the Spirit of God dwelleth in you? (1 Cor. 3:16).

If any man defile the temple of God, him shall God destroy; for the temple of God is holy, which temple ye are (1 Cor. 3:17).

Beloved, I wish above all things that thou mayest prosper and be in health, even as thy soul prospereth (3 John 2).

Bless the Lord, O my soul, and forget not all his benefits: . . . who healeth all thy diseases (Ps. 103:2-3).

. . . pray one for another, that ye may be healed. The effectual fervent prayer of a righteous man availeth much (Jas. 5:16).

What? Know ye not that your body is the temple of the Holy Ghost, which is in you, which ye have of God, . . . therefore glorify God in your body (1 Cor. 6:19-20).

. . . so now also Christ shall be magnified in my body, . . . For to me to live is Christ (Phil. 1:20-21).

. . . for ye are the temple of the living God; as God hath said, I will dwell in them, and walk in them, and I will be their God, and they shall be my people (2 Cor. 6:16).

Heaven

Is there really a heaven? Who goes there? What is it like there?

Beloved, now are we the sons of God, and it doth not yet appear what we shall be: but we know that, when he shall appear, we shall be like him; for we shall see him as he is (1 John 3:2).

For now we see through a glass, darkly; but then face to face: now I know in part; but then shall I know even as also I am known (1 Cor. 13:12).

Father, I will that they also, whom thou hast given me, be with me where I am; that they may behold my glory, which thou hast given me: for thou lovedst me before the foundation of the world (John 17:24).

In my Father's house are many mansions: if it were not so, I would have told you. I go to prepare a place for you. And if I go and prepare a place for you, I will come again, and receive you unto myself; that where I am, there ye may be also (John 14:2-3).

But as it is written, Eye hath not seen, nor ear heard, neither have entered into the heart of man, the things which God hath prepared for them that love him (1 Cor. 2:9).

But now they desire a better country, that is, an

heavenly: wherefore God is not ashamed to be called their God: for he hath prepared for them a city (Heb. 11:16).

For our conversation is in heaven; from whence also we look for the Savior, the Lord Jesus Christ: Who shall change our vile body, that it may be fashioned like unto his glorious body, according to the working whereby he is able even to subdue all things unto himself (Phil. 3:20-21).

When Christ, who is our life, shall appear, then shall ye also appear with him in glory (Col. 3:4).

For the Lord himself shall descend from heaven with a shout, with the voice of the archangel, and with the trump of God: and the dead in Christ shall rise first: Then we which are alive and remain shall be caught up together with them in the clouds, to meet the Lord in the air: and so shall we ever be with the Lord. (1 Thess. 4:16-17).

And I John saw the holy city, new Jerusalem, coming down from God out of heaven, prepared as a bride adorned for her husband. And I heard a great voice out of heaven saying, Behold, the tabernacle of God is with men, and he will dwell with them, and they shall be his people, and God himself shall be with them, and be their God. And God shall wipe away all tears from their eyes: and there shall be no more death neither sorrow, nor crying, neither shall there be any more pain: for the former things are passed away (Rev. 21:2-4).

. . . rejoice, because your names are written in heaven (Luke 10:20).

Hell

Is there really a hell? Who goes there? What is it like there?

Your Daily Walk with Christ

The Son of man shall send forth his angels, and they shall gather out of his kingdom all things that offend, and them which do iniquity; and shall cast them into a furnace of fire: there shall be wailing and gnashing of teeth (Matt. 13:41-42).

And fear not them which kill the body, but are not able to kill the soul: but rather fear him which is able to destroy both soul and body in hell (Matt. 10:28).

Marvel not at this: for the hour is coming, in the which all that are in the graves shall hear his voice, and shall come forth; they that have done good, unto the resurrection of life; and they that have done evil, unto the resurrection of damnation (John 5:28-29).

And before him shall be gathered all nations: and he shall separate them one from another, as a shepherd divideth his sheep from the goats: (Matt. 25:32).

And then will I profess unto them, I never knew you: depart from me, ye that work iniquity (Matt. 7:23).

And these shall go away into everlasting punishment: but the righteous into life eternal (Matt. 25:46).

And the devil that deceived them was cast into the lake of fire and brimstone, where the beast and false prophet are, and shall be tormented day and night for ever and ever . . . and whosoever was not found written in the book of life was cast into the lake of fire (Rev. 20:10,15).

And to you who are troubled rest with us, when the Lord Jesus shall be revealed from heaven with his mighty angels, In flaming fire taking vengence on them that know not God, and that obey not the gospel of our Lord Jesus Christ: Who shall be punished with everlasting destruction from the presence of the Lord, and from the glory of his power (2 Thess. 1:7-9).

And many of them that sleep in the dust of the earth shall awake, some to everlasting life, and some to shame and everlasting contempt (Dan. 12:2).

For if God spared not the angels that sinned, but cast them down to hell, and delivered them into chains of darkness, to be reserved unto judgment . . . The Lord knoweth how to deliver the godly out of temptation, and to reserve the unjust unto the day of judgment to be punished (2 Pet. 2:4, 9).

Holy Spirit

Who is the Holy Spirit? What is He like?

And I will put my Spirit within you, and cause you to walk in my statutes and ye shall keep my judgments, and do them (Ezek. 36:27).

Even the Spirit of truth; whom the world cannot receive, because it seeth him not, neither knoweth him: but ye know him; for he dwelleth with you, and shall be in you (John 14:17).

And it shall come to pass afterward, that I will pour out my spirit upon all flesh; and your sons and your daughters shall prophesy, your old men shall dream dreams, your young men shall see visions (Joel 2:28).

But ye shall receive power, after that the Holy Ghost is come upon you: and ye shall be witnesses unto me both in Jerusalem, and in all Judea, and in Samaria, and unto the uttermost part of the earth (Acts 1:8).

Howbeit when he, the Spirit of truth, is come, he will guide you into all truth: for he shall not speak of himself; but whatsoever he shall hear, that shall he speak: and he will show you things to come (John 16:13).

Your Daily Walk with Christ

But the Comforter, which is the Holy Ghost, whom the Father will send in my name, he shall teach you all things, and bring all things to your remembrance, whatsoever I have said unto you (John 14:26).

The Spirit itself beareth witness with our Spirit, that we are the children of God (Rom. 8:16).

But if the spirit of him that raised up Jesus from the dead dwell in you, he that raised up Christ from the dead shall also quicken your mortal bodies by his Spirit that dwelleth in you (Rom. 8:11).

Nevertheless I tell you the truth; It is expedient for you that I go away: for if I go not away, the Comforter will not come unto you; but if I depart, I will send him unto you. And when he is come, he will reprove the world of sin, and of righteousness, and of judgement: (John 16:7-8).

Hope

Hope is what keeps us keeping on. How does hope give us strength?

For we are saved by hope: but hope that is seen is not hope: for what a man seeth, why doth he yet hope for? (Rom. 8:24).

For the hope which is laid up for you in heaven, whereof ye heard before in the word of the truth of the gospel; (Col. 1:5).

Behold, the eye of the Lord is upon them that fear him, upon them that hope in his mercy (Ps. 33:18).

Why art thou cast down, O my soul? and why art thou disquieted within me? hope thou in God: for I shall yet praise him, who is the health of my countenance, and my God (Ps. 42:11).

But I would not have you to be ignorant, brethren, concerning them which are asleep, that ye sorrow not, even as others which have no hope.

For the Lord himself shall descend from heaven
. . . and the dead in Christ shall rise first: (1
Thess. 4:13,16).

Humility

How does humility relate to the "Me" generation? How do we develop unselfish attitudes?

By humility and the fear of the Lord are riches,
and honor, and life (Proverbs 22:4).
A man's pride shall bring him low: but honor
shall uphold the humble in spirit (Prov. 29:23).
Whosoever therefore shall humble himself as
this little child, the same is greatest in the kingdom of heaven (Matt. 18:4).
Though the Lord be high, yet hath he respect
unto the lowly (Ps. 138:6).
For whosoever exalteth himself shall be abased:
and he that humbleth himself shall be exalted
(Luke 14:11).
But he giveth more grace, wherefore he saith,
God resisteth the proud, but giveth grace unto
the humble (Jas. 4:6).
Likewise, ye younger, submit yourselves unto
the elder. Yea, all of you be subject one to another, and be clothed with humility: for God resisteth the proud, and giveth grace to the humble
(1 Peter 5:5).
Humble yourselves in the sight of the Lord, and
he shall lift you up (Jas. 4:10).
The Lord is nigh unto them that are of a broken
heart; and saveth such as be of a contrite spirit
(Ps. 34:18).

Joy

In everyone's life there is much pain. How do
we find continuing joy?

Then he said unto them, Go your way, eat the

fat, and drink the sweet, and send portions unto them for whom nothing is prepared: . . . for the joy of the Lord is your strength (Neh. 8:10).

For his anger endureth but a moment; in his favor is life: weeping may endure for a night, but joy cometh in the morning (Ps. 30:5).

They that sow in tears shall reap in joy (Ps. 126:5).

And the ransomed of the Lord shall return, and come to Zion with songs and everlasting joy upon their heads: they shall obtain joy and gladness, and sorrow and sighing shall flee away (Isa. 35:10).

Hitherto have ye asked nothing in my name: ask, and ye shall receive, that your joy may be full (John 16:24).

For the kingdom of God is not meat and drink; but righteousness, and peace, and joy in the Holy Ghost (Rom. 14:17).

But rejoice, inasmuch as ye are partakers of Christ's sufferings; that, when his glory shall be revealed, ye may be glad with exceeding joy (1 Pet. 4:13).

And he that reapeth receiveth wages, and gathereth fruit unto life eternal: that both he that soweth and he that reapeth may rejoice together (John 4:36).

My meditation of him shall be sweet: I will be glad in the Lord (Ps. 104:34).

Judgment

How can a just, merciful and loving God send judgment upon His own creation? How does a Christian answer this question?

I said in mine heart, God shall judge the righteous and the wicked: for there is a time there for every purpose and for every work (Eccl. 3:17).

. . . God shall judge the secrets of men by Jesus Christ according to my gospel (Rom. 2:16).

But why dost thou judge thy brother? or why dost thou set at nought thy brother? for we shall all stand before the judgment seat of Christ (Rom. 14:10).

I charge thee therefore before God, and the Lord Jesus Christ, who shall judge the quick and dead at his appearing and his kingdom. Preach the word; be instant in season, out of season, reprove, rebuke, exhort with all longsuffering and doctrine (2 Tim. 4:1-2).

But God is the judge: he putteth down one, and setteth up another (Ps. 75:7).

Say among the heathen that the Lord reigneth: the world also shall be established that it shall not be moved: he shall judge the people righteously (Ps. 96:10).

Herein is our love made perfect, that we may have boldness in the day of judgment: because as he is, so are we in this world (1 John 4:17).

But the heavens and the earth, which are now, by the same word are kept in store, reserved unto fire against the day of judgment and perdition of ungodly men (2 Pet. 3:7).

And to you who are troubled rest with us, when the Lord Jesus shall be revealed from heaven with his mighty angels . . . and that obey not the gospel of our Lord Jesus Christ (2 Thess. 1:7-8).

For the Father judgeth no man, but hath committed all judgment unto the Son (John 5:22).

Love

It is love that makes the world go around. What is involved in Christian love?

By this shall all men know that ye are my disciples, if ye have love one to another (John 13:35).

Your Daily Walk with Christ

As the Father hath loved me, so have I loved you: continue ye in my love (John 15:9).

Who shall separate us from the love of Christ? shall tribulation or distress, or persection, or famine, or nakedness, or peril, or sword? (Rom. 8:35).

Grace be with all them that love our Lord Jesus Christ in sincerity (Eph. 6:24).

But God, who is rich in mercy, for his great love wherewith he loved us, Even when we were dead in sins, hath quickened us together with Christ (Eph. 2:4-5).

For God so loved the world that he gave his only begotten Son, that whosoever believeth in him shall not perish but have everlasting life (John 3:16).

Keep yourselves in the love of God, looking for the mercy of our Lord Jesus Christ unto eternal life (Jude 21).

And we have known and believed the love that God hath to us. God is love; and he that dwelleth in love dwelleth in God, and God in him (1 John 4:16).

O love the Lord, all ye his saints: for the Lord preserveth the faithful, and plentifully rewards the proud doer (Ps. 31:23).

Ye have heard that it hath been said, thou shalt love thy neighbor, and hate thine enemy. But I say unto you, Love your enemies, bless them that curse you, do good to them that hate you, and pray for them which despitefully use you, and persecute you; that ye may be the children of your Father which is in heaven: for he maketh his sun to rise on the evil and on the good, and sendeth rain on the just and the unjust. For if ye love them which love you, what reward have ye? (Matt. 5:43-46).

And he answering said, thou shalt love the Lord thy God with all thy heart, and with all thy soul, and with all thy strength, and with all thy mind: and thy neighbor as thyself. And he said unto him, Thou has answered right: This do, and thou shalt live (Luke 10:27-28).

Obeying God

Lord, what shall I do? I want to please You.

Now therefore, if ye will obey my voice indeed, and keep my covenant, then ye shall be a peculiar treasure unto me above all people: for all the earth is mine (Ex. 19:5).
And if thou wilt walk in my ways, to keep my statutes and my commandments, as thy Father David did walk, then I will lengthen thy days (1 Kings 3:14).
For whosoever shall do the will of God, the same is my brother, and my sister, and mother (Mark 3:35).
. . . Blessed are they that hear the word of God, and keep it (Luke 11:28).
Jesus answered and said unto him, If a man love me, he will keep my words: and my Father will love him, and will come unto him, and make our abode with him (John 14:23).
Come now, and let us reason together, saith the Lord: though your sins be as scarlet, they shall be as white as snow; though they be red like crimson, they shall be as wool. If ye be willing and obedient, ye shall eat the good of the land (Isa. 1:18-19).
If ye keep my commandments, ye shall abide in my love; even as I have kept my Father's commandments, and abide in his love (John 15:10).
. . . We ought to obey God rather than men. The God of our fathers raised up Jesus, whom ye slew and hanged on a tree. Him hath God exalted with his right hand to be a Prince and a Saviour, for to give repentance to Israel, and

forgiveness of sins. And we are his witnesses of these things; and so is also the Holy Ghost, whom God hath given to them that obey him (Acts 5:29-32).

Behold, I set before you this day a blessing and a curse; a blessing if ye obey the commandments of the Lord your God, which I command you this day: and a curse, if ye will not obey the commandments of the Lord your God, but turn aside out of the way which I command you this day, to go after other gods, which ye have not known (Deut. 11:26-28).

Patience

Patience goes against the grain of human nature. Why should a Christian develop patience?

I waited patiently for the Lord; and he inclined unto me, and heard my cry (Ps. 40:1).

And it shall be said in that day, Lo, this is our God; we have waited for him, and he will save us: this is the Lord: we have waited for him, we will be glad and rejoice in his salvation (Isa. 25:9).

In your patience possess ye your souls (Luke 21:19).

Now we exhort you, brethren, warn them that are unruly, comfort the feebleminded, support the weak, be patient toward all men . . . and the very God of peace sanctify you wholly (1 Thess. 5:14,23).

And the servant of the Lord must not strive; but be gentle unto all men, apt to teach, patient, In meekness instructing those that oppose themselves; . . . that they may recover themselves out of the snare of the devil (2 Tim. 2:24-26).

For ye have need of patience, that after ye have done the will of God, ye might receive the promise. For yet a little while, and he that shall come will come (Heb. 10:36-37).

But let patience have her perfect work, that ye may be perfect and entire, wanting nothing (Jas. 1:4).

For whatsoever things were written aforetime were written for our learning, that we through patience and comfort of the scriptures might have hope. Now the God of patience and consolation grant you to be likeminded one toward another according to Christ Jesus (Rom. 15:4-5).

. . . we glory in tribulations also: knowing that tribulation worketh patience; and patience, experience (Rom. 5:3-4).

Peace

Why am I so disturbed sometimes? What is the pathway to peace?

Thus saith the Lord, Stand ye in the ways, and see, and ask for the old paths, where is the good way, and walk therein, and ye shall find rest for your souls (Jer. 6:16).

And into whatsoever house ye enter, first say, Peace be to this house. And if the son of peace be there, your peace shall rest upon it (Luke 10:5-6).

I will both lay me down in peace, and sleep: for thou, Lord only makest me dwell in safety (Ps. 4:8).

The Lord will give strength unto his people; the Lord will bless his people with peace (Ps. 29:11).

Great peace have they which love thy law: and nothing shall offend them (Ps. 119:165).

Thou wilt keep him in perfect peace, whose mind is stayed on thee: because he trusteth in thee (Isa. 26:3).

O that thou hadst hearkened to my commandments! then had thy peace been as a river, and thy righteousness as the waves of the sea (Isa. 48:18).

Peace I leave with you, my peace I give unto you: not as the world giveth, give I unto you. Let not your heart be troubled, neither let it be afraid (John 14:27).

These things have I spoken unto you, that in me ye might have peace. In the world ye shall have tribulation: but be of good cheer; I have overcome the world (John 16:33).

And the peace of God, which passeth all understanding, shall keep your hearts and minds through Christ Jesus (Phil. 4:7).

Therefore being justified by faith, we have peace with God through our Lord Jesus Christ (Rom. 5:1).

For he is our peace, who hath made both one, and hath broken down the middle wall of partition between us (Eph. 2:14).

Prayer

Does God really answer prayer?

And I say unto you, ask, and it shall be given you; seek, and ye shall find; knock, and it shall be opened unto you (Luke 11:9).

And whatsoever ye shall ask in my name, that will I do that the Father may be glorified in the Son. If ye shall ask anything in my name, I will do it (John 14:13-14).

And it shall come to pass, that before they call, I will answer; and while they are yet speaking, I will hear (Isa. 65:24).

Call unto me, and I will answer thee, and show thee great and mighty things, which thou knowest not (Jer. 33:3).

If ye abide in me, and my words abide in you,

ye shall ask what ye will, and it shall be done unto you (John 15:7).

And whatsoever we ask, we receive of him, because we keep his commandments, and do those things that are pleasing in his sight (1 John 3:22).

Confess your faults one to another, and pray one for another, that ye may be healed. The effectual fervent prayer of a righteous man availeth much (Jas. 5:16).

And ye shall seek me, and find me, when ye shall search for me with all your heart (Jer. 29:13).

If my people, which are called by name, shall humble themselves, and pray, and seek my face, and turn from their wicked ways, then will I hear from heaven, and will forgive their sin, and will heal their land (2 Chron. 7:14).

And this is the confidence that we have in him, that, if we ask anything according to his will, he heareth us; and if we know that he hear us, whatsoever we ask, we know we have the petitions that we desired of him (1 John 5:14-15).

The righteous cry, and the Lord heareth, and delivereth them out of all their troubles (Ps. 34:-17).

The Lord is far from the wicked: but he heareth the prayer of the righteous (Prov. 15:29).

Therefore I will look unto the Lord; I will wait for the God of my salvation; my God will hear me (Mic. 7:7).

Reward

The reward system is highly promoted in psychology today. Rewards are as timeless as God's plan for persons. How does God reward His children?

And they that be wise shall shine as the brightness of the firmament; and they that turn many

Your Daily Walk with Christ

to righteousness as the stars for ever and ever (Dan. 12:3).

For the Son of man shall come in the glory of his father with his angels; and then he shall reward every man according to his works (Matt. 16:27).

Now he that planteth and he that watereth are one: and every man shall receive his own reward according to his own labor (1 Cor. 3:8).

But this I say, He which soweth sparingly shall reap also sparingly; and he which soweth bountifully shall reap also bountifully (2 Cor. 9:6).

And, behold, I come quickly; and my reward is with me, to give every man according as his work shall be (Rev. 22:12).

The judgments of the Lord are true and righteous altogether . . . Moreover by them is thy servant warned: and in keeping of them there is great reward (Ps. 19:9,11).

So that a man may say, verily there is a reward for the righteous; verily he is a God that judgeth in the earth (Ps. 58:11).

And when the chief Shepherd shall appear, ye shall receive a crown of glory that fadeth not away (1 Pet. 5:4).

His lord said unto him, well done, good and faithful servant; thou hast been faithful over a few things, I will make thee ruler over many things: enter thou into the joy of thy lord (Matt. 25:23).

Henceforth there is laid up for me a crown of righteousness which the Lord, the righteous judge, shall give me at that day: and not to me only, but unto all them also that love his appearing (2 Tim. 4:8).

But lay up for yourselves treasures in heaven, where neither moth nor rust doth corrupt, and where thieves do not break through and steal (Matt. 6:20).

Service

Are there promises to God's workers?

Bear ye one another's burdens, and so fulfil the law of Christ ... As we have therefore opportunity, let us do good unto all men, especially unto them who are of the household of faith (Gal. 6:2,10).

And ye shall serve the Lord your God, and he shall bless thy bread, and thy water; and I will take sickness away from the midst of thee (Ex. 23:25).

Therefore, my beloved brethren, be ye stedfast, unmoveable, always abounding in the work of the Lord, forasmuch as ye know that your labour is not in vain in the Lord (1 Cor. 15:58).

... work out your own salvation with fear and trembling. For it is God which worketh in you both to will and to do of his good pleasure (Phil. 2:12-13).

... For unto whomsoever much is given, of him shall be much required: and to whom men have committed much, of him they will ask the more (Luke 12:48).

He also that had received two talents came and said, Lord, thou deliveredst unto me two talents: behold, I have gained two other talents beside them. His Lord said unto him, well done, good and faithful servant; thou hast been faithful over a few things, I will make thee ruler over many things: enter thou into the joy of thy Lord (Matt. 25:22-23).

... What doth the Lord thy God require of thee, but to fear the Lord thy God, to walk in all his ways, and to love him, and to serve the Lord thy God with all thy heart and with all thy soul. To keep the commandments of the Lord, and his statutes, which I command thee this day for thy good (Deut. 10:12-13).

And whosoever shall give to drink unto one of these little ones a cup of cold water only in the name of a disciple, verily I say unto you, he shall in no wise lose his reward (Matt. 10:42).

Let us not be weary in well-doing; for in due season we shall reap, if we faint not (Gal. 6:9).

Wherefore we labour, that, whether present or absent, we may be accepted of him (2 Cor. 5:9).

Whatsoever thy hand findeth to do, do it with all thy might for there is no work, nor device, nor knowledge, nor wisdom, in the grave (Eccl. 9:10).

Cast thy bread upon the waters: for thou shalt find it after many days (Eccl. 11:1).

. . . but whosoever will be great among you, shall be your minister: and whosoever of you will be the chiefest, shall be servant of all (Mark 10:43-44).

For whether is greater, he that sitteth at meat or he that serveth? is not he that sitteth at meat? But I am among you as he that serveth (Luke 22:27).

For whosoever shall give you a cup of water to drink in my name, because ye belong to Christ, Verily I say unto you, he shall not lose his reward (Mark 9:41).

Sin

What exactly is sin? What does God say about it?

Let the wicked forsake his way, and the unrighteous man his thoughts: and let him return unto the Lord, and he will have mercy upon him; and to our God, for he will abundantly pardon. (Isa. 55:7).

For the wages of sin is death; but the gift of God

is eternal life through Jesus Christ our Lord (Rom. 6:23).

Behold, all souls are mine; as the soul of the father, so also the soul of the son is mine: the soul that sinneth, it shall die (Ezek. 18:4).

Who is a God like unto thee, that pardoneth iniquity, and passeth by the transgression of the remnant of his heritage? he retaineth not his anger for ever, because he delighteth in mercy (Mic. 7:18).

If we confess our sins, he is faithful and just to forgive us our sins, and to cleanse us from all unrighteousness (1 John 1:9).

Repent ye therefore, and be converted, that your sins may be blotted out, when the times of refreshing shall come from the presence of the Lord (Acts 3:19).

Draw nigh to God, and he will draw nigh to you. Cleanse your hands, ye sinners; and purify your hearts, ye doubleminded (Jas. 4:8).

For thou art not a God that hath pleasure in wickedness: neither shall evil dwell with thee. The foolish shall not stand in thy sight: Thou hatest all the workers of iniquity (Ps. 5:4-5).

If I regard iniquity in my heart, the Lord will not hear me: (Ps. 66:18).

As righteousness tendeth to life, so he that pursueth evil pursueth it to his own death (Prov. 11:19).

My little children, these things write I unto you, that ye sin not. And if any man sin, we have an advocate with the Father, Jesus Christ the righteous (1 John 2:1).

Soul-winning

Many people feel inadequate as soul-winners. What promises does God give to the one who wins souls?

And they that be wise shall shine as the brightness of the firmament; and they that turn many to righteousness as the stars for ever and ever (Dan. 12:3).

The fruit of the righteous is a tree of life; and he that winneth souls is wise (Prov. 11:30).

And he saith unto them, Follow me, and I will make you fishers of men (Matt. 4:19).

Let him know, that he which converteth the sinner from the error of his way shall save a soul from death, and shall hide a multitude of sins (Jas. 5:20).

To the weak became I as weak, that I might gain the weak: I am made all things to all men, that I might by all means save some (1 Cor. 9:22).

Therefore saith he unto them, the harvest truly is great, but the laborers are few: pray ye therefore the Lord of the harvest, that he would send forth laborers into his harvest (Luke 10:2).

Say not ye, there are yet four months, and then cometh harvest? behold, I say unto you, lift up your eyes, and look on the fields, for they are white already to harvest. And he that reapeth receiveth wages, and gathereth fruit unto life eternal; that both he that saveth and he that reapeth may rejoice together (John 4:35-36).

They that sow in tears shall reap in joy. He that goeth forth and weepeth, bearing precious seed, shall doubtless come again with rejoicing, bringing his sheaves with him (Ps. 126:5-6).

He that is not with me is against me: and he that gathereth not with me scattereth abroad (Matt. 12:30).

Speech

Cursing and bad language are very common today. What promises does God give to the person who keeps his speech clean?

Whoso keepeth his mouth and his tongue, keepeth his soul from troubles (Prov. 21:23).

A man hath joy by the answer of his mouth; and a word spoken in due season, how good is it (Prov. 15:23).

Thou shalt not take the name of the Lord thy God in vain; for the Lord will not hold him guiltless that taketh his name in vain (Ex. 20:7).

Pleasant words are as a honeycomb, sweet to the soul, and health to the bones (Prov. 16:24).

For in many things we offend all. If any man offend not in word, the same . . . is able to bridle the whole body (Jas. 3:2).

The words of a wise man's mouth are gracious; but the lips of a fool will swallow up himself (Eccl. 10:12).

The Lord God hath given me the tongue of the learned, that I should know how to speak a word in season to him that is weary: he wakeneth morning by morning, he wakeneth mine ear to hear as the learned (Isa. 50:4).

Let your speech be always with grace, seasoned with salt, that ye may know how ye ought to answer every man (Col. 4:6).

But I say unto you, that every idle word that men shall give account thereof in the day of judgment (Matt. 12:36).

Strength

God has always promised strength to His followers. What kinds of strength has He promised?

In that day shall the Lord of hosts be for a crown of glory, and for a diadem of beauty, unto the residue of his people, and for a spirit of judgment to him that sitteth in judgment, and for strength to them that turn the battle to the gate (Isa. 28:5-6).

Your Daily Walk with Christ

But they that wait upon the Lord shall renew their strength; they shall mount up with wings as eagles; they shall run, and not be weary; and they shall walk, and not faint (Isa. 40:31).

Fear thou not; for I am with thee: be not dismayed; for I am thy God: I will strengthen thee: yea, I will help thee; yea, I will uphold thee with the right hand of my righteousness (Isa. 41:10).

And such as do wickedly against the covenant shall be corrupt by flatteries: but the people that do know their God shall be strong, and do exploits (Dan. 11:32).

That ye might walk worthy of the Lord unto all pleasing, being fruitful in every good work, and increasing in the knowledge of God; Strengthened with all might, according to his glorious power, unto all patience and longsuffering with joyfulness (Col. 1:10-11).

And he said unto me, my grace is sufficient for thee: for my strength is made perfect in weakness. Most gladly therefore will I rather glory in my infirimities, that the power of Christ may rest upon me (2 Cor. 12:9).

The Lord is my strength and my shield; my heart trusted in him, and I am helped (Ps. 28:7).

God is our refuge and strength, a very present help in trouble (Ps. 46:1).

My flesh and my heart faileth: but God is the strength of my heart, and my portion forever (Ps. 73:26).

Behold, God is my salvation; I will trust, and not be afraid: for the Lord Jehovah is my strength and my song; he also is become my salvation (Isa. 12:2).

I can do all things through Christ which strengtheneth me (Phil 4:13).

Success

Success is usually considered a worldly trait. What kind of success does the Bible promise Christians?

My God shall supply all your need according to his riches in glory by Christ Jesus (Phil. 4:19).

Therefore take no thought, saying, what shall we eat? Or what shall we drink? or where withal shall we be clothed? . . . for your heavenly Father knoweth that ye have need of all these things (Matt. 6:31-33).

But seek ye first the kingdom of God, and his righteousness; and all these things shall be added into you (Matt. 6:33).

For where your treasure is, there will your heart be also (Matt. 6:21).

. . . a man's life consisteth not in the abundance of the things which he passesseth (Luke 12:15).

But what things were gain to me, those I counted loss for Christ (Phil 3:7).

Boast not thyself of tomorrow; for thou knowest not what a day may bring forth (Prov. 27:1).

The Lord is my shepherd; I shall not want (Ps. 23:1).

. . . If riches increase, set not your heart upon them. God hath spoken once; twice have I heard this; that power belongeth unto God (Ps. 62:10-11).

If I have made gold my hope, . . . If I rejoiced because my wealth was great, . . . This also were an iniquity to be punished by the judge: for I should have denied the God that is above (Job 31:24-25,28).

Your Daily Walk with Christ

Suffering

Blessed are ye, when man shall revile you, and persecute you, and shall say all manner of evil against you falsely, for my sake (Matt. 5:11).

And ye shall be hated of all men for my name's sake: but he that endureth to the end shall be saved (Matt. 10:22).

He that findeth his life shall lose it: and he that loseth his life for my sake shall find it (Matt. 10:39).

And if children, then heirs; heirs of God, and joint heirs with Christ; if so be that we suffer with him, that we may be also glorified together (Rom. 8:17).

For what glory is it, if when ye be buffeted for your faults, ye shall take it patiently? but if, when ye do well, and suffer for it, ye take it patiently, This is acceptable with God (1 Pet. 2:20).

For as the sufferings of Christ abound in us, so our consolation also aboundeth by Christ . . . and our hope of you is steadfast, knowing, that as ye are partakers of the sufferings, so shall ye also of the consolation (2 Cor. 1:5,7).

If we suffer, we shall also reign with him: if we deny him, he also will deny us: (2 Tim. 2:12).

If ye be reproached for the name of Christ, happy are ye; for the spirit of glory and of God resteth upon you: . . . if any man suffer as a Christian, let him not be ashamed (1 Pet. 4:14,16).

And every one that hath forsaken houses, or brethren, or sisters, or father, or mother or wife, or children, or lands, for my name's sake, shall receive a hundredfold, and shall inherit everlasting life (Matt. 19:29).

Many are the afflictions of the righteous: but the Lord delivereth him out of them all (Ps. 34:19).

For I reckon that the sufferings of this present time are not worthy to be compared with the glory which shall be revealed in us (Rom. 8:18).

Therefore I take pleasure in infirmities, in reproaches, in necessities, in persecutions, in distress for Christ's sake: for when I am weak, then am I strong (2 Cor. 12:10).

For our light affliction, which is but for a moment, worketh for us a far more exceeding and eternal weight of glory (2 Cor. 4:17).

Temptation

Temptations are a fact of life. How do we go about overcoming them?

There hath no temptation taken you but such as is common to man: but God is faithful, who will not suffer you to be tempted above that ye are able; but will with the temptation also make a way to escape, that ye may be able to bear it (1 Cor. 10:13).

For in that he himself hath suffered being tempted, he is able to succour them that are tempted (Heb. 2:18).

My brethren, count it all joy when ye fall into divers temptations; knowing this, that the trying of your faith worketh patience (Jas. 1:2-3).

Blessed is the man that endureth temptation: for when he is tried, he shall receive the crown of life, which the Lord hath promised to them that love him. (Jas. 1:12).

The Lord knoweth how to deliver the godly out of temptation, and to reserve the unjust unto the day of judgment to be punished (2 Pet. 2:9).

Wherefore take unto you the whole armour of God, that ye may be able to withstand in the evil day, and having done all, to stand. Stand therefore, having your loins girt about with truth, and having on the breastplate of righteousness; and your feet shod with the preparation of the gospel of peace; above all, taking the shield of faith, wherewith ye shall be able to quench all the fiery darts of the wicked. And take the helmet of salvation, and sword of the Spirit, which is the word of God (Eph. 6:13-17).

Submit yourselves therefore to God. Resist the devil, and he will flee from you. (Jas. 4:7).

Ye are of God, little children and have overcome them: because greater is he that is in you, than he that is in the world (1 John 4:4).

He is like a man which built a house, and digged deep, and laid the foundation on a rock: and when the flood arose, the stream beat vehemently upon that house, and could not shake it; for it was founded upon a rock (Luke 6:48).

Time

Time is one of the most precious gifts of God. How can we use it profitably?

Lord, thou hast been our dwelling place in all generations . . . thou turnest man to destruction, and sayest, Return, ye children of men. For a thousand years in thy sight are but as yesterday when it is past, and as a watch in the night . . . The days of our years are threescore years and ten: and if by reason of strength they be fourscore years, yet is their strength labour and sorrow; for it is soon cut off, and we fly away . . . So teach us to number our days, that we may apply our hearts unto wisdom (Ps. 90:1,3-4, 10,12).

Whereas ye know not what shall be on the morrow. For what is your life? It is even a vapour, that appeareth for a little time, and then vanisheth away . . . Therefore to him that knoweth to do good, and doeth it not, to him it is sin. (Jas. 4:14,17)

Bible Promises for Growing Christians

the Lord, which made heaven and earth (Ps. 121:1-2).

. . . but if any man be a worshipper of God, and doeth his will, him he heareth (John 9:31).

I went into the sanctuary of God; then understood I (Ps. 73:17).

My meditation of him shall be sweet: I will be glad in the Lord (Ps. 104:34).

Acquaint now thyself with him and be at peace: thereby good shall come unto thee (Job 22:21).

Delight thyself also in the Lord; and he shall give thee the desires of thine heart (Ps. 37:4).

Test Yourself

He that is slow to _____ is better than the mighty; (Prov. 16:32).

For our gospel came not in word only, but also in power, and in the Holy Ghost, and in much _____; (1 Thess. 1:5).

All _____ is given by inspiration of God, and is profitable for doctrine, for reproof, for correction, for instruction in righteousness (2 Tim. 3:16).

In the world ye shall have tribulation; but be of good _____; I have overcome the world (John 16:33).

For _____ is the end of the law for righteousness to every one that believeth (Rom. 10:4).

Wait on the Lord: be of good _____, and he shall strengthen thine heart: wait, I say, on the Lord (Ps. 27:14).

Those that be planted in the _____ shall flourish in the courts of our God (Ps. 92:13).

He that overcometh shall inherit all things; and I will be his God, and he shall be my son (Rev. 21:7).

For to me to live is Christ, and to _____, is gain (Phil 1:21).

And the Lord, he it is that doth go before thee;

Your Daily Walk with Christ

he will be with thee, he will not fail thee, nor forsake thee: fear not, neither be _____. (Deut. 31:8).

If you have faith and _____ not, ye shall say unto this mountain, Be thou removed, and be thou cast into the sea; it shall be done (Matt. 21:21).

Fear God, and Keep his commandments: for this is the whole _____ of man. For God shall bring every work into judgment, with every secret thing, whether it be good, or whether it be evil (Eccl. 12:13-14).

But without _____ it is impossible to please him: for he that cometh to God must believe that he is, and that he is a rewarder of them that diligently seek him (Heb. 11:6).

Honor thy _____ and _____ which is the first commandment with promise; that it may be well with thee, and thou mayest live long on the earth. (Eph. 6:2-3).

For if ye _____ men their tresspasses, your heavenly Father will also _____ you: (Matt. 6:14).

A man that hath _____ must show himself friendly; and there is a _____ that sticketh closer than a brother (Prov. 18:24).

Every man according as he purposeth in his heart, so let him _____; not grudgingly, or of necessity: for God loveth a cheerful _____ (2 Cor. 9:7).

In every thing give _____: for this is the will of God in Christ concerning you. (1 Thess. 5:18).

As newborn babes, desire the sincere milk of the word, that ye may _____ thereby: (1 Pet. 2:2).

Know ye not that ye are the _____, and that the Spirit of God dwelleth in you. (1 Cor. 3:16).

Rejoice, because your names are written in _____ (Luke. 10:20).

Bible Promises for Growing Christians

And fear not them which kill the body, but are not able to kill the soul: but rather fear him which is able to destroy both body and soul in _____ (Matt. 10:28).

But the Comforter, which is the _____, whom the Father will send in my name, he shall teach you all things, and bring all things to your remembrance, whatsoever I have said unto you (John 14:26).

For we are saved by _____: but _____ that is seen is not _____: for what a man seeth, why doth he yet _____ for? (Rom. 8:24).

But he giveth more grace wherefore he saith, God resisteth the proud, but giveth grace unto the _____ (Jas. 4:6).

They that sow in tears shall reap in _____ (Ps. 126:5).

But why dost thou _____ thy brother? or why dost thou set at nought thy brother? for we shall all stand before the _____ seat of Christ? (Rom. 14:10).

God is _____: and he that dwelleth in _____ dwelleth in God, and God in him (1 John 4:16).

If ye _____ my commandments, ye shall abide in my love (John 15:10).

I waited _____ for the Lord; and he inclined unto me; and heard my cry. (Ps. 40:1).

Thou wilt keep him in perfect _____, whose mind is stayed on thee: because he trusteth in thee. (Isa. 26:3).

The effectual fervent _____ of a righteous man availeth much (Jas. 5:16).

Now he that planteth and he that watereth are one: and every man shall receive his own _____ according to his own labor (1 Cor. 3:8).

Whosoever will be great among you, shall be

Your Daily Walk with Christ

your minister: and whosoever of you will be chiefest, shall be _____ of all (Mark 10:43-44).

For the wages of _____ is death; but the gift of God is eternal life through Jesus Christ our Lord (Rom. 6:23).

The fruit of the righteous is a tree of life: and he that winneth _____ is wise (Prov. 11:30).

If any man offend not in _____: the same is a perfect man, and able also to bridle the whole body (Jas. 3:2).

But they that wait upon the Lord shall review their _____; they shall mount up with wings as eagles; they shall run, and not be weary; and they shall walk, and not faint (Isa. 40:31).

If we _____ we shall also reign with him: if we deny him, he also will deny us: (2 Tim. 2:12).

Blessed is the man that endureth _____: for when he is tried, he shall receive the crown of life, which the Lord hath promised to them that love him. (Jas. 1:12).

For he saith, I have heard thee in a _____ accepted, and in the day of salvation have I succoured thee: behold now is the accepted _____; behold now is the day of salvation (2 Cor. 6:2).

The lip of _____ shall be established for ever: but a lying tongue is but for a moment (Prov. 12:19).

Give unto the Lord due his name: bring an offering, and come before him: _____ the Lord in the beauty of holiness. Fear before him, all the earth: the world also shall be stable, that it be not moved (1 Chron. 16:29-30).

III
God's Promises Through Spiritual Exercises

How to Have a Quiet Time with God

The person who enjoys a quiet time alone with God each day is practicing a long and rich Christian tradition. Jesus set the pattern for such a time when He "was alone praying" (Luke 9:18) on occasions Jesus "withdrew himself in the wilderness and prayed"; (Luke 5:16) "went up into a mountain apart to pray"; (Matt. 14:23) withdrew from his disciples "about a stone's cast, and kneeled down, and prayed"; (Luke 22:-41) "went out, and departed into a solitary place, and there prayed" (Mark 1:35).

The purpose of a quiet time with God is to focus attention upon the God's plan for your life. Jesus did not withdraw from life. His quiet time was an opportunity to mediatate upon God's presence in the midst of problems, perils, and possibilities. A daily quiet time links our life to God and God to all of our life. It allows us time to contemplate upon our faith in God, to demonstrate our reverence for God and to enjoy our Father-child relationship with God. It is an indispensable practice for the growing Christian.

Practical Aids to a Quiet Time

I. Set a definite time. The Gospel writer records that Jesus enjoyed a quiet time in the morning, "rising up a great while before day (Mark 1:35). Another time Jesus "departed into a mountain to pray . . . when evening was come" (Mark 6:46-47). Choose the time that is best for your schedule. The benefits of an early morning quiet

Spiritual Exercises

time are: feeling refreshed from a night's rest, a quiet household, allows prayer for coming daily activities.

II. Select a definite place. It should be a place where you can be relatively free from interruptions.

III. Select a devotional guide for your quiet time. Some helps available are: (a) Read the Bible through in a year; (b) *Home Life* Devotions; (c) *Open Windows* Devotions; (d) Sunday School or Church Training daily Bible readings.

IV. Set prayer goals for your quiet time. Study the topics listed in Part II for forming your goals.

V. Have materials available

    a. Bible—choose the version which fits your devotional needs: King James Version, *New American Standard,* Revised Standard Version, *The Good News, The Living Bible*

    b. Notebook and pencil to list prayer concern and answered prayers.

    c. A dated devotional guide.

VI. Devotional Exercises Review
    Your definite time;
    Your definite place;
    Your devotional guide;
    Your prayer goals;
    Your quiet-time materials.

How to Pray

Prayer is a communion of a person with God through a merger of your will into His will. It is the best preparation you can make for anything you fear—conflict, sorrow, duty, or joy. God's promises to the prayerful person are manifold. Study the prayer promises given in Chapter II. Prayers is composed of thanksgiving, praise, confession, petition, and intercession. Follow this spiritual exercises to effective prayer.

Bible Promises for Growing Christians

I. Thank God for His goodness. Mention specifically the ways you have been blessed—health, home, family, friends, finances, salvation.

II. Praise God for His nature. Thank Him for His attitude and actions toward you. God is:

a.	loving	1 John 4:8
b.	merciful	Ps. 116:5
c.	mighty	Job 36:5
d.	faithful	1 Cor. 1:9
e.	true	John 3:33
f.	holy	Ps. 99:9
g.	light	1 John 1:5
h.	great	Job 36:26

III. Confess all sins before God. Ask for His forgiveness of daily sins. Confess sins against those in your family. Confess sins against those in your church. Confess sins against neighbors. Confess sins against those with whom you work. Confess sins of the mind. Confess sins of the tongue.

IV. Petition God for your daily needs: personal, family, physical, career, spiritual, social.

V. Intercede with God on behalf of others. Intercessory prayer should be definite. Moses, David and Hezekiah are examples of people who prayed for others. Moses—Ex. 32:32; David—1 Chron. 21:17; Hezekiah—2 Chron. 30:18.

Write the name of one unsaved person you will pray for this year.

Write the name of one Christian that has fallen away from God that you will pray for this year.

Write the name of a person or family with physical needs that you will pray for and minister to this year.

Write the name of a person or family with

Spiritual Exercises

emotional needs that you will pray for and minister to this year.

Pick at least one worldwide or international need. Pray regularly and specifically for the people who face these threats: nuclear destruction, world hunger, wars of aggression, or other disasters.

Write the names of spiritual leaders you should pray for on a regular basis. Do not forget your pastor.

Write the name of a person to whom you have difficulty relating. Pray for him or her daily.

How to Find God's Will in Your Life

Throughout the Bible we are promised that seeking the Lord will bring knowledge of His will for our life. Some of God's greatest promises are:

But if . . . thou shalt seek the Lord thy God, thou shalt find him, if thou seek him with all thy heart and with all thy soul (Deut. 4:29).

I love them that love me; and those that seek me early shall find me (Prov. 8:17).

Seek ye the Lord while he may be found, call ye upon him while he is near: (Isa. 55:6).

But without faith it is impossible to please him: for he that cometh to God must believe that he is, and that he is a rewarder of them that diligently seek him (Hebrews 11:6).

Careful examination of these promises reveals several steps to finding the will of God.

I. Desire—the spiritual seeker desires to find God's will. It is an all-consuming desire; one that demands the total surrender of our heart and soul (Deut. 4:29).

II. Dedication—if our love is sincere toward God, he has promised to return that love and reveal himself to us (Prov. 8:17).

Bible Promises for Growing Christians

Tell God that you love Him. Tell Him why you love Him. List the reasons for your love on a separate sheet of paper.

III. Determination—finding God's will requires a commitment to seek open eyes and hearts all of the ways, times, and people through which God may speak. check below. (See Prov. 8:17).

I will "early" seek to know God's will in the time of: sorrow, crises, needs, joy.

IV. Directions—to find the direction of God's will for our life, we must have a beginning point. That beginning point is faith (Heb. 11:6).

Do you believe that if you follow God's direction to seek Him, you will know His will?

What does it mean to believe that God exists?

In what ways will God give you directions? See Prov.3:6, Ps.23:2, Ps.25:9, Ps. 48:14, John 16:13.

How to Lead a Person to Christ

I. The A-B-C Plan of Salvation. Focus upon the key words in each Scripture verse. memorize the plan. Point out God's promises of salvation to these who sin and are willing to trust Jesus for forgiveness.

a. For *all* have sinned and come short of the glory of God, (Rom. 3:23).
b. *Believe* on the Lord Jesus Christ and thou shalt be saved (Acts 16:31).
c. That if thou shalt *confess* with thy mouth the Lord Jesus, and shalt believe in thine heart that God hath raised him from the dead, thou shalt be saved (Rom. 10:9).

II. The Roman Road plan of Salvation. These progressive verses from the Book of Romans will lead a person to Christ.

Spiritual Exercises

a. For all have sinned and come short of the glory of God (Rom. 3:23). This shows the universality of sin.
b. But God commendeth his love toward us, in that while we were yet sinners, Christ died for us (Rom. 5:8). This shows God's love for sinful persons.
c. For the wages of sin is death; but the gift of God is eternal life through Jesus Christ our Lord (Rom. 6:23). This shows both sin's gift to us and God's gift to us.
d. There is therefore now no condemnation to them which are in Christ Jesus, who walk not after the flesh, but after the Spirit (Rom. 8:1). This shows God will not condemn those who trust in Christ.
e. That if thou shalt confess with thy mouth the Lord Jesus, and shalt believe in thine heart that God hath raised him from the dead, thou shalt be saved (Rom. 10:9). This shows that a person must trust Christ privately in his heart and publicly with his mouth.
f. For whosoever shall call upon the name of the Lord shall be saved (Rom. 10:13). This is God's promise to everyone.
g. I beseech you therefore, brethren, by the mercies of God, that ye present your bodies a living sacrifice, holy, acceptable unto God, which is your reasonable service. And be not conformed to this world: but be ye transformed by the renewing of your mind, that ye may prove what is that good, and acceptable, and perfect, will of God (Rom. 12:1-2). This shows that the new Christian must follow God's leadership every day.

III. The story of salvation in one verse: For God so loved the world, that he gave his only begot-

ten son, that whosoever believeth in him should not perish, but have everlasting life (John 3:16).
a. God's love—for everyone in the world.
b. God's sacrifice—His son died for everyone.
c. God's plan—trust in His son's sacrifice.
d. God's promise—everlasting life

IV. The salvation experience of Nicodemus and Zacchaeus
a. Nicodemus—John 3:1-21
   1. Nicodemus came to Jesus (3:2).
   2. Jesus knew his need (3:2).
   3. Jesus explained "new birth" (3:14-18).
   4. Jesus invited Nicodemus to experience "new birth" (3:14-18).
b. Zacchaeus—Luke 19:1-10
   1. Zacchaeus came to Jesus (10:1-4).
   2. Jesus knew his need (19:5).
   3. Zacchaeus repented of sins (19:8).
   4. Salvation came to Zacchaeus (19:9-10).

V. A testimony of your own salvation experience. Write it out on a separate sheet

Use your testimony to tell others how to be saved.

List persons by name on a separate sheet with whom you want to share God's promises about salvation.

Here are some suggested persons with whom to share salvation promises: mother, father, brother(s), sister(s), son(s), daughter(s), neighbor(s), teacher(s), doctor, grocery store clerk(s), nurse.

How to Memorize Scripture

Many people in times of great trials have testified to the strengthening power of memorized Bible verses. Soldiers in battle, prisoners of war, persons experiencing great physical, mental,

Spiritual Exercises

emotional, and spiritual stress have all felt the comfort of memorized Scripture. The psalmist felt that strength when he wrote, "Thy word have I hid in mine heart, that I might not sin against thee" (Ps. 119:11).

Memorizing one of God's promises each week is a good discipline for the growing Christian. Fifty-two Bible promises are listed herein for your use. Follow the steps below in memorizing one each week.

I. Memorize a verse as a family at mealtime devotional. Read it aloud in unison. Take turns quoting it to each other. If you live alone, read the promise aloud to yourself. Work at memorizing it.

II. Quote the verse aloud to yourself at least twice at bedtime each night.

III. Write the verse on a strip of paper and attach it to the front of your refrigerator with a magnetic holder. Study it each time you open your refrigerator.

IV. Enclose a copy of the Scripture promise in your pocket or purse. Think of it each time you make a purchase.

V. Memorize a verse in partnership with a friend each week. Think of ways that Scripture memory can make you a better friend. Practice each other's verse.

VI. Jot down a brief thought on the meaning of the Bible promise to your life.

Jesus memorized Scripture. It was this ability that allowed Him to refute and defeat Satan in the wilderness temptation (Matt. 4:1-11).

Scripture memorization is a vital part of Christian growth.

Bible Promises for Growing Christians

Scripture Memory

A Promise for Every Week of the Year

As you read these weekly Scripture selections, write on a separate sheet of paper in brief what each passage has meant to your life as the words have become a part of of it.

1. For God so loved the world that he gave his only begotten Son, that whosoever believeth in him should not perish, but have everlasting life (John 3:16).
2. For the wages of sin is death; but the gift of God is eternal life through Jesus Christ our Lord (Rom. 6:23).
3. For by grace are ye saved through faith; and that not of yourselves: it is the gift of God (Eph. 2:8).
4. I can do all things through Christ which strengtheneth me (Phil. 4:13).
5. And the peace of God, which passeth all understanding shall keep your hearts and minds through Christ Jesus (Phil 4:7).
6. Blessed is the man that endureth temptation: for when he is tried, he shall receive the crown of life, which the Lord hath promised to them that love him (Jas. 1:12).
7. Ask and it shall be given you; seek, and ye shall find; knock, and it shall be opened unto you (Matt. 7:7).
8. The Lord is my shepherd; I shall not want (Ps. 23:1).
9. The Lord is my light and my salvation; whom shall I fear? The Lord is the strength of my life; of whom shall I be afraid (Ps. 27:1).
10. Blessed is the nation whose God is the Lord (Ps. 33:12).
11. I sought the Lord, and he heard me, and delivered me from all my fears (Ps. 34:4).

Spiritual Exercises

12. Restore unto me the joy of thy salvation; and uphold me with thy free spirit. Then will I teach trangressors thy ways; and sinners shall be converted unto thee (Ps. 51:12-13).
13. It is more blessed to give than to receive (Acts 20:35).
14. And all things, whatsoever ye shall ask in prayer, believing, ye shall receive (Matt. 21:22).
15. Verily, I say unto you, Except ye be converted, and become as little children, ye shall not enter into the Kingdom of heaven (Matt. 18:3).
16. For whosoever will save his life shall lose it: and whosoever will lose his life for my sake shall find it (Matt. 16:25).
17. Come unto me, all ye that labor and are heavy laden, and I will give you rest (Matt. 11:28).
18. Whosoever shall confess me before men, him will I confess also before my father which is in heaven (Matt. 10:32).
19. And fear not them which kill the body, but are not able to kill the soul: but rather fear him which is able to destroy both soul and body in hell (Matt. 10:28).
20. Not every one that saith unto me, Lord, Lord, shall enter into the kingdom of heaven; but he that doeth the will of my father which is in heaven (Matt. 7:21).
21. Follow me, and I will make you fishers of men (Matt. 4:19).
22. And I give unto them eternal life; and they shall never perish, neither shall any man pluck them out of my hand (John 10:28).
23. And whosoever liveth and believeth in me shall never die (John 11:26).
24. I am the way, the truth, and the life: no man

Bible Promises for Growing Christians

cometh unto the Father, but by me (John 14:6).

25. Go ye therefore, and teach all nations, baptizing them in the name of the Father, and of the Son, and of the Holy Ghost: Teaching them to observe all things whatsoever I have commanded you: and lo, I am with you alway, even unto the end of the world (Matt. 28:19-20).

26. I am the vine, ye are the branches. He that abideth in me, and I in him, the same bringeth forth much fruit: (John 15:5).

27. There is therefore now no condemnation to them which are in Christ Jesus, . . . (Rom. 8:1).

28. And we know that all things work together for good to them that love God, to them who are the called according to his purpose (Rom. 8:28).

29. But God commandeth his love toward us, in that, while we were yet sinners, Christ died for us (Rom. 5:8).

30. For to be carnally minded is death; but to be spiritually minded is life and peace (Rom. 8:6).

31. If God be for us, who can be against us? (Rom. 8:31).

32. For whosoever shall call upon the name of the Lord shall be saved (Rom. 10:13).

33. Know ye not that ye are the temple of God, and that the Spirit of God dwelleth in you (1 Cor. 3:16)?

34. Upon the first day of the week let every one of you lay by him in store, as God hath prospered him (1 Cor. 16:2).

35. For we know that if our earthly house of this tabernacle were dissolved, we have a building of God, a house not made with hands, eternal in the heavens (2 Cor. 5:1).

Spiritual Exercises

36. ... Walk in the Spirit, and ye shall not fulfill the lusts of the flesh. (Gal. 5:16).
37. Be not deceived; God is not mocked: for whatsoever a man soweth, that shall he also reap (Gal. 6:7).
38. Now unto him that is able to do exceeding abundantly all that we ask or think, according to the power that worketh in us (Eph. 3:20).
39. And be ye kind one to another, tenderhearted, forgiving one another, even as God for Christ's sake hath forgiven you (Eph. 4:32).
40. Put on the whole armor of God, that ye may be able to stand against the wiles of the devil (Eph. 6:11).
41. For if we believe that Jesus died and rose again, even so them also which sleep in Jesus will God bring with him (1 Thess 4:14).
42. For whom the Lord loveth he chasteneth, and scourgeth every son whom he receiveth (Heb. 12:6).
43. If any of you lack wisdom, let him ask of God, that giveth to all men liberally, and upbraideth not; and it shall be given him (Jas. 1:5).
44. Humble yourselves in the sight of the Lord, and he shall lift you up (Jas. 4:10).
45. ... The effectual fervent prayer of a righteous man availeth much. (Jas. 5:16).
46. Beloved now are we the sons of God, and it doth not yet appear what we shall be like him (1 John 3:2).
47. A soft answer turneth away wrath: but grevious words stir up anger (Prov. 15:1).
48. But they that wait upon the Lord shall renew their strength, they shall mount up with wings as eagles; they shall run, and not be weary; and they shall walk, and not faint (Isa. 40:31).

Bible Promises for Growing Christians

49. Call unto me, and I will answer thee, and show thee great and mighty things, which thou knowest not (Jer. 33:3).
50. Bring ye all the tithes into the storehouse, that there may be meat in mine house, and prove me now herewith, saith the Lord of hosts, if I will not open you the windows of heaven, and pour you out a blessing, that there shall not be room enough to receive it (Mal. 3:10).
51. He that believeth on me hath everlasting life (John 6:47).
52. Thanks be unto God for his unspeakable gift (2 Cor. 9:15).

How to Get Along with Others

Getting along with others is very important in every area of life. When God created persons with the freedom to choose, He created a world of people with differing opinions, desires, goals and interests. This diversity makes the world a very interesting place. It is also helps to cause wars, arguments, jealousies, injustice, and many other unpleasant events.

I. What does the Bible have to teach about getting along with others of God's creation? Here are instances of human relations in the Bible. How did the people involved solve their problems?

1. Abraham and Lot—Gen. 13:1-12.

The servants of Abraham (uncle) and Lot (nephew) disagreed over whose animals should get the best grazing land.

2. Jacob and Esau—Gen. 27:18-41 and 32:6 to 33:15.

The younger brother Jacob used deceit to get a blessing from their father Issac which was rightfully due the older brother Esau.

Spiritual Exercises

3. David and Absalom—2. Sam. 13:19 to 18:19.

An ambitious young man wanted to become king of Israel even if it meant the death of his father King David.

4. Jesus and His family—Mark 3:31-35.

The family of Jesus did not understand His ministry and sought to persuade Him to come back home.

5. Mary and Martha—Luke 10:38-42.

Martha complained about the apparent laziness of her sister Mary.

6. Paul, Barnabas, and John Mark—Acts 15:36-41.

Paul and Barnabas had a serious argument over the future ministry of Barnabas's nephew Mark who had deserted them on a missionary journey.

II. List specific problems in your family, in your work place, in your school, in your church.

III. Develop a plan for improving relationships with the people involved in these problems. Include in your plan prayer Bible study, conversation with the persons involved, applying biblical principles to relationships, and faith that God can improve the situation.

IV. Principles for Human Relations: follow the Golden Rule, turn the other cheek, love your enemies, show yourself friendly, be a good neighbor, do more than is required.

How to Live Through Difficult Times

Motto: Life and death, blessing and cursing, therefore choose life (Deut. 30:19).

Difficult times come to all of us sooner or later. How we face and overcome these difficulties depends upon our belief in God's promises.

Bible Promises for Growing Christians

Consider these suggestions and exercises as aids to strengthen your faith.

I. *Make a conscious choice to live victoriously every day. Jesus said of His followers:* I am come that they might have life, and that they might have it more abundantly (John 10:10). No matter what difficult situations touch your life, you can hold to Christ's promise.

II. *Trust God to know your limits. God will not allow more to come upon you than you can bear.* There hath no temptation taken you but such as is common to man: but God is faithful, who will not suffer you to be tempted above that ye are able; but will with the temptation also make a way to escape, that ye may be able to bear it (1 Cor. 10:13). Read Job's story in the Old Testament. Job was tormented by his closest friends and advised by his wife to curse God and die. He had lost his property, his health, and his children. Job replied: Though He (God) slay me, yet will I trust him. . . (Job 13:15). His attitude was not determined by the events of life but by his trust in God.

III. *Claim the promise of victorious living that God offers His children.* One man of you shall chase a thousand: for the Lord your God, he it is that fighteth for you, as he hath promised you (Joshua 23:10). And he said unto me, my grace is sufficient for thee: for my strength is made perfect in weakness. Most gladly therefore will I rather glory in my infirmities that the power of Christ may rest upon me. (2 Cor. 12:9).

IV. *Read these Bible stories of people who lived through difficulties.*

1. Abraham—Genesis 12-23
2. Joseph—Genesis 37-50

Spiritual Exercises

3. Moses—Exodus 2-6
4. Jeremiah—Jeremiah 26, 37
5. Daniel—Daniel 1-6
6. John Mark—Acts 13-15
7. Paul—Acts 16, 21-28
8. Jesus—The Gospel of John

Difficulties will come. But, they will also pass. God wants to help you in all circumstances, on all occasions, especially in your difficult times.

How to Get the Most out of Life

God promises heaven for all His followers after this life is over (Rev. 21-22). He also promises to give good gifts to His children that will make this life abundant, victorious, happy, and joyful.

Galatians 5:22-23 lists God's gifts: But the fruit of the Spirit is love, joy, peace, longsuffering, gentleness, goodness, faith, meekness, temperance: against such there is no law.

I. Consider each gift separately. Write how you can use this gift to enrich your life and glorify God. Be specific.
   Look up the meaning of each of these words in a good Bible dictionary.
II. Consult a Bible concordance to read aloud verses which use these terms. Claim them as God's gifts to you. As you meditate upon each one, some gifts will appear as clusters of heavenly fruit waiting for you to gather. Other promised gifts will appear as blank checks signed by God for you to cash.
III. Read a biography of a Christian whose life exemplifies these gifts. Consult your church library or Christian book store for suggestions.
IV. Claim these gifts as God's promises to you. Practice them in your daily living. Choose

one gift to practice each week for nine consecutive weeks. Ask God's guidance daily.

Getting the most out of life depends upon attitude, not circumstances. Life is a precious gift. Cherish every moment of it. Practice the habit of doing daily deeds of kindness to others. Delight in the beauty of nature. Smile at people. Be positive in all things. Happiness is being God's child, living in God's world, following God's will.